IMPRESSIONS of the

CHILTERNS

Produced by AA Publishing

Published by AA Publishing (a trading name of AA Media Limited, whose registered office is Fanum House, Basing View, Basingstoke, Hampshire RG21 4EA; registered number 06112600)

ISBN: 978-0-7495-6411-7

A04066

A CIP catalogue record for this book is available from the British Library.

Printed and bound in China by C & C Offset Printing Co. Ltd

Opposite: Hughenden Valley, north of High Wycombe, Buckinghamshire, epitomises the beech-dominated, steep-sided valleys of the Chilterns. Prime Minister Benjamin Disraeli lived here for 40 years until his death in 1881.

IMPRESSIONS of the

CHILTERNS

Picture Acknowledgements

The Automobile Association would like to thank the following photographers, companies and picture libraries for their assistance in the preparation of this book.

Abbreviations for the picture credits are as follows: (t) top; (b) bottom; (l) left; (r) right; (AA) AA World Travel Library.

3 John Prior Images/Alamy; 5 Jason Gallier/Alamy; 7 Robert Stainforth/Alamy; 8 Robert Harding Picture Library Ltd/Alamy; 9 AA/J Tims; 10 Jason Gallier/Alamy; 11 Jason Gallier/Alamy; 12 Tom Mackie/Alamy; 13 The Big Sky Photography/Alamy; 14 Adam Ward/Alamy; 15 Gary Curtis/Alamy; 16 Robert Stainforth/Alamy; 17 Renee Morris/Alamy; 18 Graham Uney/Alamy; 19 Sam Vaughan/Alamy; 20 Nick Jenkins/Alamy; 21 Dennis Chang – UK/Alamy; 22 Robert Stainforth/Alamy; 23 Robert Harding Picture Library Ltd/Alamy; 24 JEVGENIJA/Alamy; 25 Chris Howes/Wild Places Photography/Alamy; 26 dov makabaw/Alamy; 27 dov makabaw/Alamy; 28 Nick Jenkins/Alamy; 29 Mark Beton/Alamy; 30 Pretty Pictures/Alamy; 31 Tim Gainey/Alamy; 32 ImagesEurope/Alamy; 33 david martyn hughes/Alamy; 34 AA/J Tims; 35 AA/J Tims ; 36 Tim Graham/Alamy; 37 Robert Stainforth/Alamy; 38 Vicki Wagner/Alamy; 39 AA/J Tims; 40 Greg Balfour Evans/Alamy; 41 AA/J Tims; 42 Paul Felix Photography/Alamy; 43 Colin Underhill/Alamy; 44 Nikreates/Alamy; 45 dov makabaw/Alamy; 46 david martyn hughes/Alamy; 47 Photofrenetic/Alamy; 48 Robert Stainforth/Alamy; 49 Elizabeth Debenham/Alamy; 50 Adam Ward/Alamy; 51 david martyn hughes/Alamy; 52 Gordon Morrison/Alamy; 53 AA/J Tims; 54 Greg Balfour Evans/Alamy; 55 Greg Balfour Evans/Alamy; 56 Dunstone Images/Alamy; 57 Photofrenetic/Alamy; 58 Alasdair Ogilvie/Alamy; 59 one-image photography/Alamy; 60 Vicki Wagner/Alamy; 61 Robert Stainforth/Alamy; 62 AA/J Tims; 63 Oxford Picture Library/Alamy; 64 Avico Ltd/Alamy; 65 david martyn hughes/Alamy; 66 Jason Gallier/Alamy; 67 CRPhoto/Alamy; 68 Neil Setchfield/Alamy; 69 Chris Rose/BlueSkyStock/Alamy; 70 Colin Underhill/Alamy; 71 CRPhoto/Alamy; 72 Graham Uney/Alamy; 73 Jeremy Trew;Trewimage/Alamy; 74 Robert Stainforth/Alamy; 75 Jo Chambers/Alamy; 76 Mark Beton/Alamy; 77 Chiltern Image Service/Alamy; 78 Paul Felix Photography/Alamy; 79 Jason Gallier/Alamy; 80 Matt Jones/Alamy; 81 Peter Packer/Alamy; 82 John Prior Images/Alamy; 83 Greg Balfour Evans/Alamy; 84 Robert Stainforth/Alamy; 85 Robert Stainforth/Alamy; 86 Robert Marshall,VividVisions Online Gallery/Alamy; 87 Robert Stainforth/Alamy; 88 Avico Ltd/Alamy; 89 Robert Stainforth/Alamy; 90 Paul Debois/Alamy; 91 Mark Beton/Alamy; 92 David Chapman/Alamy; 93 BlueSkyStock/Alamy; 94 Caroline Jones/Alamy; 95 John Prior Images/Alamy.

Every effort has been made to trace the copyright holders, and we apologise in advance for any accidental errors. We would be happy to apply any corrections in the following edition of this publication.

Opposite: A traditional 17th-century post mill – one of the oldest in England – stands sentinel in fields between the villages of Pitstone and Ivinghoe.

INTRODUCTION

'Surely the finest landscape within an hour of central London': this glowing description of the Chilterns comes not from one of Michael Palin's travelogues, or from John Betjeman's documentary *Metro-land* (though Metroland is always nudging into the Chilterns!) It comes from Oxford-based author Ian McEwan in his dark, psychological fictional thriller *Enduring Love*.

Fiction blurs into fact however, because the Chiltern Hills do lie only a few miles to the north-west of London and yet have a totally rural character. Rising to over 850 feet they feel ancient and even prehistoric (and indeed there are the remains of many prehistoric hill forts dotted along the ridges). Dominated by huge stands of beech woods, the Chilterns run in a 50-mile curve from the Thames and stretch north-east through Buckinghamshire and Bedfordshire to Hitchin in Hertfordshire. Where the hills fall away in dramatic style down the steep-sided slopes into the Thames Valley, they become nature's crumpled wall, shutting off London from the Cotswolds and beyond. It began just 10,000 years ago when the chalk and flint backbone of the Chiltern escarpment was exposed by melting glaciers leaking into the clay deposits of the plain below. Fast forward and an early 7th-century manuscript still bewailed the solitude and desolation of the Chiltern hills whose steep contours remained for many centuries a barrier to communication and travel.

That has all changed with the M40 motorway. Today most people whiz through the Chilterns without knowing it, following signs to High Wycombe, Oxford, and beyond. They descend via the deep cutting in the chalk hills that carries the motorway out of the Chilterns – its stark off-white gash now the dominant feature of the buttressed landscape.

To enjoy the gentle rigours of the Chilterns, you definitely need to detour, preferably with a knapsack, map and flask. Park the car and follow the exposed footpaths and ramblers' routes – not least the ancient Ridgeway and Icknield Way that crisscross the Chilterns. Officially, the Ridgeway Walk runs 87 miles from Overton Hill in Wiltshire to Ivinghoe Beacon near Tring, crossing five counties. The Chiltern Hills section follows the prehistoric trails used by hunters, gatherers, herdsmen, and skirmishers along the chalk ridge. The key attraction of the Chilterns, however, lies on the other side of the tracks, as it were, deep inside the heavily wooded clumps and stands of beech, oak and ash. Walk into the dappled light, under the swaying canopy of the radiantly green beeches, and you'll trample along velvety carpets of piled up beech leaves and nuts. As the trees sway to the breeze like creaking machinery you might catch a glimpse of fallow deer and away from the dark woods you will hear the *mew mew* of red kites soaring above on the thermals. The once endangered bird of prey has almost become the mascot of the Chilterns, so many are their number since billionaire Sir Paul Getty reintroduced the birds at Wormsley, his 3,000-acre Chilterns estate.

And for those seeking more human contact, there are plenty of rural flint-and red brick towns such as Marlowe, West Wycombe, and Wendover, and villages including Ewelme, Turville (where *The Vicar of Dibley* was filmed) and Hambledon offering eye-catching cottages, manor houses, and churches as well as weirs and windmills. Inside *Impressions of the Chilterns* you'll find beautifully captured images of both the natural and manmade sights that make up the rugged rural retreat that is the Chilterns.

Opposite: Rape fields lend an almost savannah-like colour to the countryside around the large chalk lion etched into a spur of the Chiltern hills at Dunstable Downs. The lion marks the site of Whipsnade Zoo, famous for its breeding programmes and cheetahs.

One of the best ways to see the Chilterns is by narrowboat along the Thames or via the Grand Union Canal.

Opposite: Nestled in the valley of the Chilterns, the white-timbered Hambledon Mill, named in 1338, has a weathervane resting on its turret.

A fallow deer buck is disturbed under the beech canopy – the Chiltern woodlands are home to several large deer populations.

Commonly found in birch woods in autumn, the large red cap and white warts of the Fly agaric mushroom are a warning sign of poison.

Resembling a Loire Valley chateau, Waddesdon Manor lies west of Aylesbury. Built in 1880-9 by a Frenchman for the Rothschilds, the property houses a famous collection of French furniture and fine Sèvres porcelain.

An exposed ridge of the Chiltern hills rises out of flat farmland – in this instance the jarringly-bright yellow fields of oil seed rape.

A field of poppies dominate the early summer landscape along the high-level route to Ivinghoe Beacon.

The ancient windmill between Pitstone and Ivinghoe. This type of 'post mill' was built around a single post that could be turned around to catch the prevailing wind.

Sheep graze on the undulating fields by Wendover Woods, against a backdrop of some of the most breathtaking scenery in Buckinghamshire.

Located where the Icknield Way meets the London to Aylesbury road, the charming Chiltern village of Wendover has an array of attractive whitewashed, half-timbered thatched-roofed cottages.

A signpost highlights two ancient long-distance footpaths: the Ridgeway and Icknield Way. The Ridgeway route runs for 87 miles.
Opposite: The ancient track of Icknield Way rises to 560 feet at Deacon Hill, providing commanding views over Bedfordshire.

A great golden ball sits atop the red brick-and-flint St Lawrence's Church in West Wycombe. It was built by Sir Thomas Dashwood, founder of the notorious rakish Hellfire Club. They met in the tower allegedly to practise black magic.

Head out of the beech woods and at the edge of the Chilterns, the broad Vale of Aylesbury spreads out in rich pastureland with many dairy farms.

Sunset at Tring Reservoirs, Hertfordshire, a haven for birdlife at the northern end of the Chilterns and surrounded by canals on three sides.

Nestled in a rich downland, the village of Turville in the heart of the Chilterns was used as the fictional village for the popular TV comedy The Vicar of Dibley.

The highest point of the Chilterns, Coombe Hill at 852 feet, is marked by this 1904 obelisk dedicated 'to the wars in South Africa'.
Opposite: Ivanhoe Beacon at 730 feet is one of the highest spots on the Chilterns and was a prehistoric hillfort. Beacons were lit here as an early warning system from Roman times through to the Spanish Armada and World War II – hence the name.

On the Chiltern plateau, Turville Heath provides an idyllic meander. It boasts an avenue of pollarded lime trees.

Turville's quirky brick and flintstone structures include this dormered cottage complete with an extremely crooked chimney stack.

West Wycombe, after Amersham, is architecturally the most satisfying Chiltern town. In its heyday it was a furniture-making centre based on the abundant supplies of good timber from the famous local beech woods.

The gently rolling hills of the Chilterns form an impressive ridge as they rise from the low farmlands of the Thames Valley.

St Mary the Virgin Church dates from the 14th century and dominates the historic village of Hambleden nestled in a narrow valley of the Chilterns.

*The distinctive blue patch across its narrow ridge identifies the fly orchid (*Ophrys insectifera*) which is found in the Chilterns.*

An aerial view of the ancient Ridgeway Path set against the modern giant U-turn indentations of a combine harvester at Ivanhoe.
Opposite: The simple grandeur of the Pitstone windmill set amidst a cornfield with Ivinghoe Beacon in the background.

Geese, ducks and swans jostle for tidbits along the Thames with Marlow's eye-catching suspension bridge and imposing All Saints Church in the distance.

Detail of a plaque on Marlow's famous suspension bridge that marks the boundary between Berkshire and Buckinghamshire. Swans have royal protection along the Thames.

If one domestic architectural feature sums up the Chilterns, it is the red brick-and-flint façaded houses, of which this is a fine example.

Picturesque Hambledon village with church and 15th-century manor house nestled beside mixed woodland dominated by beech. The church tower was rebuilt in 1721.

A carved seat provides ramblers' rest along the Chiltern ridge above Watlington looking over the Vale of Oxford which stretches for some 20 miles beyond.

A graceful drinking fountain in Marlow town centre is dedicated to an American theatrical producer named Charles Frohman who perished in the sinking of the Lusitania *in 1915 (and who lived in the town)*

The large 12th-century Church of St Mary's in Hemel Hemstead is one of the finest in the country. The 14th-century timber spire is almost 200 feet high.

The chunky Norman tower of Bisham church dates from 1175 and dominates this idyllic setting right on the Thames near Marlow.

In the Vale of Oxford below Watlington lie the watercress beds (now restored) at Ewelme. The old village boasts a highly attractive brick-and-flint church, school and almshouses.

Rolling pastureland mixed with wooded hillsides at Turville, and further still the Chiltern ridge bedecked with birch.

Pastureland and paddocks peter out into scrub and the chalky ridgetop of the rolling Chiltern Hills in Buckinghamshire.
Opposite: A meandering stretch of Turville Heath showing off lush buttercup-laden meadows before rising into the heavily wooded Chiltern amphitheatre.

Victorian villas and boathouses vie for dominance with the native trees on the steeply wooded Thames banks near Marlow.

A row of telegraph lines along gently rolling wheatfields at Dunstable Downs echo a vaster New World prairie landscape.

On the edge of the Chilterns, Wendover Woods provides a wintery windswept scene where three of the highest points converge – Boddington Hill, Backham Hill and crowning them both, Coombe Hill.

A Small Heath butterfly rests on ribwort plantain at Ivinghoe. The chalk base also attracts the local Chalkhill Blue butterfly.

Ivinghoe Beacon rises over 730 feet to another ancient hillfort. It is the final spur of the Chilterns downland ridge and marks the official end of the Ridgeway National Trail.

The fine spire of All Saints Church, Marlow, soars to 170 feet. The church itself is made of Staffordshire brick with Bath Stone dressings.

The velvety chalk grassland of Barton Hills is covered with wild thyme, marjoram, rockrose and orchids. The rare pasque flower comes out between April and June.
Opposite: Marlow's handsome suspension bridge (1831) was built by the same architect who designed a bridge once connecting Buda with Pest in Hungary.

Chalfont St Giles by the Misbourne brook is a pretty town in which John Milton wrote Paradise Lost. *His cottage is now a museum.*

The Ashridge Estate follows a ridge of the Chilterns for nearly a mile, providing rich views of the chalk downlands of the Vale of Aylesbury.

The Chilterns provide an ideal sojourn for boaters and walkers along the Grand Union Canal (1801) linking London with Birmingham. This bridge is at Denham Country Park.

Ivinghoe Beacon and the Chilterns beckon across this field from Pitstone.

The Henton Mission Room, a 'transportable' 50-seater chapel of timber and corrugated iron popular with missionaries, is one of 25 buildings at the Chiltern Open Air Museum, Chalfont St Giles.

A lone tree tells the age-old tale of the prevailing winds atop the Chiltern Hills.

In West Wycombe every village is a National Trust property. This half-timbered pilgrim's rest house with red brick and stucco is typical – the upper storey projects over the street with no foundations!

Opposite: Rosebay willowherb and other wild flowers frame this stunning view of the Vale of Oxford near Watlington.

From Marlow's weir the spire of All Saints Church beside the suspension bridge forms one of the most eye-catching scenes anywhere along the Thames.

Time has stood still at Ewelme nestled below the Chilterns near Watlington. Many of the buildings date back to the 15th century and the village boasts the oldest school building in the country still in use as a state primary school.

Red kites soaring on the thermals have become a common sight in the Chilterns since their reintroduction to the area.

Marsworth is the starting point for a superb six-mile canalside walk along the Grand Union Canal to Aylesbury.

A fallow deer buck with its distinctive flattened antlers. Introduced by the Normans after 1066, this is the most widespread species of deer in Britain.
Opposite: Hints of autumn advertise the edge of the Ashridge Estate – a vast swathe of beautiful woodlands and chalk downland at the north end of the Chiltern Hills between Aylesbury and Hemel Hempstead.

Jerome K. Jerome who wrote the hilarious Thames-side tale Three Men in a Boat *is buried here at St Mary's Church, Ewelme.*

Built to the design of William Tierney Clarke in 1831, the suspension bridge is Marlow's most famous feature. This stretch of the Thames sees many pretty gardens and beech trees reaching down to the water's edge.

It's not surprising that the pretty Chiltern Hills village of Turville, near High Wycombe, is a popular film and TV location.
Opposite: Sunset on the Dunstable Downs, one of the highest spots in the east of England, with outstanding views over the Vale of Aylesbury and Chiltern ridge.

A light dusting of snow covers the steep chalk hills and quiet valleys of the Pegsdon Hills in Bedfordshire. Even in winter there's a good chance to see brambling, stonechat, fieldfare and buzzards.

Halfway between High Wycombe and Aylesbury on the Chiltern escarpment lies the oldest 'smock' (because it resembles such a garment) windmill in England, built in about 1650.

There are over 350 types of sweet on offer at this sweetshop-cum-newsagent on West Wycombe's heritage High Street.

Boats for hire are moored below Marlow's handsome suspension bridge. Its main span is 235 feet long.

Terraced cottages at Turville, with the Pitstone windmill visible in the background atop the Chiltern ridge.
Opposite: In spring the bluebells provide a swaythe of stunning purples amidst the beech copses in the Chilterns.

Ewelme is famous for its watercress beds, established in the 1890s on a chalk stream running through the village. This was dammed and widened to provide large beds of shallow, slow-running water under which the cress was planted.

The windmill near Ivinghoe. From the top of the ridge here you can see the extensive line of the Chilterns, the Quainton Hills and the Dunstable Downs.

Rolling farmland below the Ivinghoe Beacon. Sir Walter Scott was inspired to name his famous novel Ivanhoe *after the area.*

You wouldn't guess that the M40 motorway lies just behind this 'curtain' of autumnal hues from beech and other trees.

504825
SQUIRREL NUTKIN

Sheep grazing in the rich pastureland valley at Maidensgrove in Oxfordshire, below the Chiltern ridge.

Opposite: A narrowboat chugs along the Grand Union Canal on the Wendover arm. This flat stretch gives little warning of the climb to come of 56 locks over 36 miles toward the Tring summit.

The beech-dominated canopy spreads right down to the river bank by this 'villa' and boathouse on the Thames near Henley.

Ivinghoe Beacon catches the morning sun as a hopeful snowboarder makes the most of a thin seasonal sprinkling.

The golden leaves of a beech tree reflect the sharp sunlight of a glorious autumn afternoon.

The London Gliding Club takes off below the Dunstable Downs, giving the flyers undoubtedly the best view of the Chilterns.

Wendover has many quaint whitewashed timbered cottages with finely thatched roofs.

Henley-on-Thames boasts this elegant 18th-century bridge.

A frosty fog covers the hinterland between the Dunstable Downs and Ivinghoe Beacon in the distance.

Pollarding, thinning and clearing are all important aspects of woodland management in the Chilterns.

*The bright purple Chiltern gentian (*Gentianella germanica*) is native only to the Chiltern Hills and is Buckinghamshire's 'county flower'.*

The wide expanse of the Thames at Marlow provides ideal rowing practise. On this stretch are Olympian oarsmen made.

Stonor Park near Henley provides a winter scene of rich timbered parkland below wood-crested hills.
Opposite: It is not hard to see why the Chilterns have been designated an 'Area of Outstanding Natural Beauty'.

INDEX